State of Vermont
Department of Libraries
Northeast Regional Library
RD 2
Box 244
St. Johnsbury, VT 05819

Keith Lye
General Editor
Henry Pluckrose

Franklin Watts
London   New York   Sydney   Toronto

Facts about Portugal

Area:
92,082 sq. km.
(35,553 sq. miles)

Population:
10,291,000

Capital:
Lisbon
Largest cities:
Lisbon (818,000)
Porto (330,000)
Amadora (94,000)
Setúbal (77,000)

Official language:
Portuguese

Religion:
Christianity

Main exports:
Textiles, machinery, timber, chemicals, cork, wine, fish

Currency:
Escudo

Franklin Watts Limited
12a Golden Square
London W1

ISBN: UK Edition 0 86 313 444 0
ISBN: US Edition 0 531 10196 7
Library of Congress Catalog
Card No: 86 50019

©Franklin Watts Limited 1986

Typeset by Ace Filmsetting Ltd,
Frome, Somerset
Printed in Hong Kong

Maps: Tony Payne

Design: Edward Kinsey

Stamps: Stanley Gibbons Limited

Photographs: Chris Fairclough, 8, 22; Portuguese National Tourist Office, 24, 26, 28; Zefa, 3, 4, 5, 6, 7, 11, 12, 14, 15, 17, 21, 23, 25, 29, 30, 31; Travel Photo International 10, 16, 27; J. Allan Cash 18, 19
Front cover: Zefa
Back cover: Portuguese National Tourist Office

Portugal is a small country in south-western Europe. It has broad coastal plains that face the Atlantic Ocean. Inland, there are uplands that extend into Spain. Portugal was once considered to be part of Spain. But it became an independent kingdom in 1143.

Lisbon, Portugal's largest city, has been the official capital since the late 13th century. The River Tagus (or Tejo) flows through Lisbon. Its estuary is one of the world's finest ports. This beautiful city has a mixture of old and new buildings.

Porto, which used to be called Oporto, is the only other large city in Portugal. The Arrábida Bridge over the River Douro in Porto is Europe's longest concrete arch bridge. Only three out of every ten people in Portugal live in cities and towns.

Portugal has a mild climate. Summers are hot and dry in the south, while winters are pleasant and moist. The north and the interior uplands are cooler and damper. The southern province of Algarve has many resorts.

Impressive cliffs of yellow rock line parts of the Algarve coast. The money spent by tourists in Portugal is now an important part of the economy. In 1983, nearly nine million tourists visited Portugal.

The picture shows some stamps and money used in Portugal. The main unit of currency is the escudo, which contains 100 centavos.

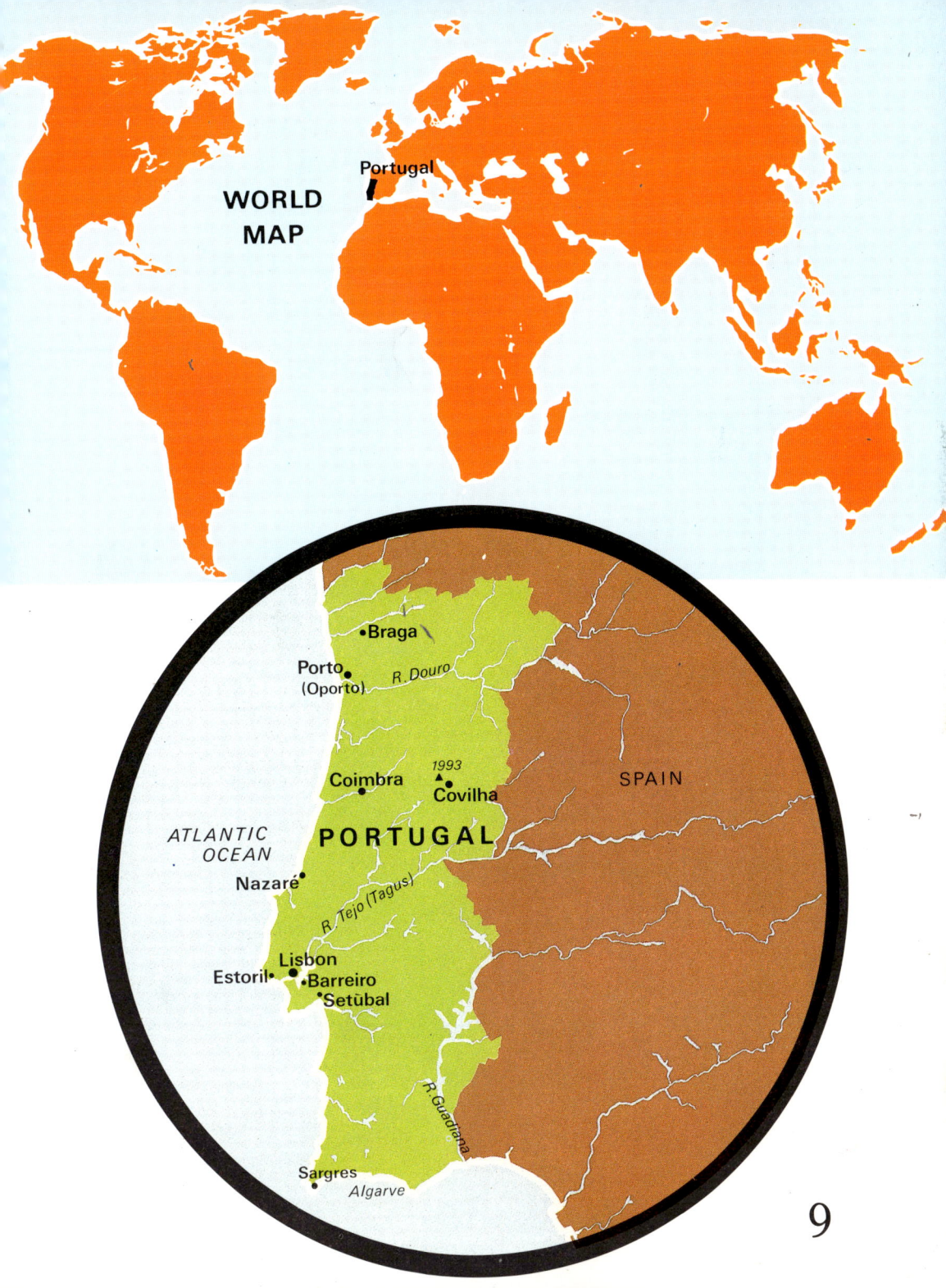

The Castle of São Jorge in Lisbon was once the home of Portugal's kings. Portugal became a republic in 1910. But in 1926, army officers took power and abolished parliament. Portugal was a dictatorship until 1974.

Portugal now has a parliament, called the Assembly of the Republic, with 250 elected members. Many government offices are housed in the buildings around the Praça do Comércio, a square in Lisbon.

About nine out of every ten people in Portugal are Roman Catholics. There are also some Jews, Muslims and Protestants. The picture shows the Church of São Vicente de Fora in Lisbon. This church was built between 1582 and 1627.

Seven out of every ten people live in small farming and fishing villages. The first people in Portugal were the Iberians. Many other peoples from Europe and North Africa settled there later. The Portuguese people today are a mixture of all these groups.

About 28 out of every 100 workers in Portugal are employed in farming, fishing and forestry. The main crops are beans, maize, oats, potatoes, rye and wheat. Vineyards and olive groves also cover large areas.

Windmills pump water to the surface and drive machines to grind grain. Many farmers have small plots and lack modern machinery. But machines are coming into use, especially on large, government-owned farms.

15

Animal rearing is especially important in northern and north-western Portugal. Portugal has more than five million sheep and nearly a million cattle. The main sheep rearing areas are in the drier uplands.

Forests cover about a third of Portugal. Pine forests grow in the north and cork oak forests in the south. The bark of cork oak trees is used to make bottle stoppers, floats and corkboard.

Grapes for making wine are grown throughout Portugal. In some places, people still use the old method of crushing grapes with their bare feet. Portugal is the world's ninth most important wine producer.

Port wine is shipped downriver from the upper Douro valley, where it is made. It is exported through the city of Porto, from which it got its name. Madeira made on the Madeira Islands is another famous Portuguese wine.

Fishing is the job of about 38,000 people in Portugal. Sardines and anchovies are caught, and cod is fished in the seas off Newfoundland, Canada by Portuguese fishermen. The picture shows fishing boats on the beach at Nazaré.

Portugal has many craft industries, including embroidery. The country has some coal and various metal ores, which are used in such industries as steelworks and shipyards. The processing of forest and farm products is also important. Industry employs about a third of Portugal's workers.

Trade is becoming more important to Portugal as the people work to raise their living standards. Portugal joined the European Economic Community, or Common Market, in 1986. It is the poorest of the 12 member countries.

Many people live in old houses, like these in Porto. Most people believe in keeping close family ties. Several generations of people often live in the same building. Many people enjoy staying up late, talking with friends.

The Portuguese people enjoy fish, including sardines and dried cod, which are often served with rice and salad. Olives and eggs are common ingredients in dishes and olive oil is used for cooking.

Coimbra is an old city which contains Portugal's oldest university, which was founded in 1290. Education is free and compulsory for children from 6 to 14 years of age. But about a fifth of adults cannot read or write.

Bullfights attract many people in Portugal. But the bulls are not killed at these bullfights, as they are in Spain. Soccer and golf are other leading pastimes in Portugal.

The country's sunny climate and the many beautiful beaches make fishing, swimming, windsurfing and other seaside activities popular sports for Portuguese people and tourists.

In the 15th century, the Portuguese Prince Henry founded a school for navigators near Sagres, on the bleak southwestern tip of Portugal. These navigators included Vasco da Gama, who sailed to India around Africa. Portugal later founded a vast empire.

Portugal's power began to decline in the 16th century. In 1822, it lost Brazil, although Portuguese is still spoken there. Portugal now has only three overseas territories. One is a group of islands, called the Azores, in the North Atlantic Ocean.

The Madeira Islands off northwestern Africa are also part of Portugal. The picture shows Madeira's capital, Funchal. Portugal withdrew from its African possessions—Angola, Cape Verde, Guinea-Bissau, Mozambique, and São Tomé and Principe—in the 1970s.

Portugal also controls the 16 sq. km. (6 sq. mile) territory of Macao, on the southeast coast of China. Although most of Portugal's empire has gone, 157 million people around the world speak Portuguese, the world's eighth most widely spoken language.

Index

Algarve 6–7
Arrábida Bridge 5
Atlantic Ocean 3, 29
Azores 29

Bullfighting 26

Castle of São Jorge 10
Climate 6
Cork 17
Coimbra 25
Crops 14

Da Gama, Vasco 28
Douro, River 5, 19

Education 25
Embroidery 21
European Economic
    Community 22

Family life 23
Farming 13–16
Fishing 20
Food 24
Forests 17
Funchal 30

Government 11

Henry, Prince 28
History 3, 10, 28–30

Industry 21

Lisbon 4, 10–12

Macao 31
Madeira 19, 30
Money 8

Nazaré 20

Pastimes 26–27
Porto 5, 19, 23
Portuguese language 31

Religion 12

Sagres 28
Sheep 16
Stamps 8

Tagus, River 4
Tourism 7, 27
Trade 7

Windmills 15
Windsurfing 27
Wine 18–19